Joy COMES IN THE Morning

Angela Tipton-Huss

ISBN
978-1-960197-04-7 (Paperback)
978-1-960197-05-4 (eBook)
978-1-960197-03-0 (Hardcover)

Joy COMES IN THE Morning

Table of Contents

Thanks to All

All praise, glory and gratitude go to my "DADDY". Thank you father God for filling the void of an absentee father. I feel blessed to have learned all that you have taught me in life. You are the source of my joy. Thank you for teaching me to hold tight to you while also letting go so that I might grow into a woman whose life could glorify you. I love you with all my heart, my mind and my soul.

Elizabeth, with your dancing eyes and compassionate spirit you gave me forgiveness and taught me about grace. You were my hope in a devastating time in my life. You continue to give me strength every day. I want to say that I love you with all my heart. I am so sorry that you found yourself lost in everyone's misery. I am so glad that we found each other again. I am sorry that we failed to remember that you were our HOPE.

Suzanna with your strong faith and your passion for doing God's will, you taught me to trust in God and let Him lead me.

Evan with your inquisitive personality and unconditional love you have given me a sense of adventure and the gift of patience.

Janet you came into our lives to teach us to surrender daily and trust our Lord completely. Janet, you allowed me the beautiful honor of being your mommy. You trusted me when the world taught you distrust. I thank God for the precious experience of being with you at the very moment you got to go and be with Jesus. Every thought of you and your brothers brings joy and happiness in place of sorrow and bleakness. Where tears abode before, now laughter resides.

Katie, with you blue eyes and beautiful smile you give such joy. Cody you are our calm after the storm. You are our rainbow, the symbol of God's promises, and the proof of His faithfulness.

To my adopted children, Suzanna, Evan, Janet, Katie, and Cody, I want to impart to you that you are loved beyond measure. You are not blood of my blood or bone of my bone, but you are the children of my heart. You abide there with your sister and brothers. You are my new beginning and the symbol of God's grace in my life.

All of my children, borne or not, have come to me on wings of angels and through God's grace, carried their mommy home from a very dark place.

I thank God every day for using my unborn children to break my heart so that I would be open to His will, and that my heart would be wide open to accept my beautiful God given children. These wonderful babies may not have grown under my heart, but they certainly grew in it.

My unborn angels, I want to express the hurt I feel that you were unable to experience life as we know it. You have forever made an impression upon our hearts and lives. I am sorry for not recognizing the significance of your little lives. Thank you, my dear, sweet sons, for bringing reality and honor to our lives through your deaths.

Mom, what do I say that would even come close? Thank you for the example you set. As I watched you struggle working and going to school I learned so much about being a mom. You taught me to work hard and sacrifice myself daily for others and to be a loving, unselfish mother to my children. You will never know how very important you have been in my life. I love you Thank you for the beautiful photo memories of my family throughout the years.

To my dear friend Leslie Richardson I want to say thank you. Your support, prayers and constructive criticism have been my life raft throughout this process. You are always there to listen and offer advise if needed, and you have the unique talent of knowing when to let things go unsaid. Thank you for helping me grow and encouraging my writing.

To our faithful friends, Robert and Mary Ann. How do I begin to thank you for the hours you have spent in prayer and service to our family. We never could have done this without you by our side. Thanks to all those who have worked and interacted with our family through the years, friends, care providers, physicians, and other professionals. Your service has never gone unnoticed.

To my wonderful, compassionate husband, I say thank you for always being my source of support. You waited patiently for me to come out of my shell. You tenderly held me and let me cry, all the while crying with me. I cherish all the times you have prayed with me and for me. I can never thank you enough for encouraging me and coming alongside me when I need you most. You are my best friend and my God appointed mate. I love you with all of my heart. None of this would have been possible without you.

To Harry and Kittie I want to say so much. The words do not come easy. Thank you seems so insignificant. Without your determination to give life to Greg and your persistence to help him lead a productive and happy life where would we all be? I would not have the honor of loving a man after God's heart. My children would not have such an amazing provider and example of their heavenly father's love. The world is a better place because you allowed God to work in your lives. Harry, thank you for standing in the place of my absent father. You have been an encourager, a prayer warrior and a daddy to me. Kittie you have taken me under your wing from the beginning never looking back. You accept our family as is and offer so much strength and encouragement. Thank you a thousand times over for loving my husband and giving him over to God. He has certainly been used for God's Glory. I love you both more than you can ever know.

Much appreciation to our friends, family and our French Broad Baptist Church family. I could not have gotten through so much without your prayer and support. Thank you for loving and accepting our family "as is". You are a true example of our Father's love for us.

A Word from the Author

It never fails to amaze me what miracles lie in the everyday experiences of life. This is the story of how very ordinary children affected my life in an extraordinary way. My husband Greg and I have been married seventeen wonderful years and we have built a unique family together. We have six terrific children. All but our oldest are adopted and have various special needs.

When we started our life together, I don't think either of us realized the path God would lead us to travel. All of our journeys with our children are unique and wonderful. But our lives were forever changed when God asked the impossible and then showed us the possibilities.

In September of 2003 God blessed us with an angel daughter. Janet was a beautiful child who captured our hearts from the first moment we laid eyes on her. Her small stature and long beautiful brown hair that almost reached the back of her knees drew you to gaze into her amazing green eyes. Those eyes will forever hold my heart. Janet could not talk, but those eyes communicated every fear, every happy thought, every giggle and all the love she felt in her heart for those around her.

We met Janet in September and knew that although there would be problems we wanted her in our family. We looked into her eyes and knew that no matter what lie ahead we were meant to be together. None of us had any way to know the enormity of what we would face as a family, or what our precious daughter would face in the year following her homecoming.

This is the story of an amazing little girl who faced adversity her entire life and left a legacy that will remain forever in the hearts of all who knew her. This is also the story of the lives she touched and the lessons she taught us. I will attempt to tell our story as honestly as I possible can. Regarding the facts about the beginning of her life, I have only records given to us about the DSS investigation and their relationship with her family. I will write from my heart and give you the facts as I know them to be.

I only hope that her story will touch you and leave you with a stronger faith, a stronger zeal for life, and the ability to love a little deeper. My prayer is that, as you get to know Janet and our family you will examine your own life and learn more about our creator as she teaches you to seek the purpose you were created for.

I also pray that you will see our Savior's providence in your own life as you watch God work in her life to provide a family for her where there was none. May you feel God's peace as you walk through our difficult journey and experience our ups and downs. Last but not least I pray that in some way God will reveal his unconditional love for you in a new and amazing way as you see the last year of our life with Janet unfold and God's plans come to completion in her life.

In Christ,
Angela

Joy Comes In the Morning

Unless the Lord builds the house, it's builders labor in vain. Unless the Lord watches over the city, the watchmen stand guard in vain. In vain you rise early and stay up late, toiling for food to eat- for he grants sleep to those he loves. Sons are a heritage to from the Lord, children are a reward from Him. Like arrows in the hands of a warrior are sons born in one's youth. Blessed is the man whose quiver is full of them. They will not be put to shame when they contend with their enemies at the gate.

Psalms 127:1-5

My Prayer

Children of my heart I pray
That you will see God's love anew in me each day.

When I awake it's with thoughts of you
And how God blesses me each anew.

With hugs, kisses and I love you,
be careful, this you don't and this you do
I journey through each wonderful day
Marveling at the miracle of God's way.

I bathe you, feed you, give you a bath.
I do your laundry, read you books and teach you math.
I dry your tears and hold you tight.
I chase away your fears at night.

When I rest my head at night
I pray fervently with all my might.

Children of my heart I pray
That you will see God's love anew in me each day.

Thank You

You came into my life
during a time of great strife.
You entered my heart
when I thought I would never love again.

You gave me a reason to believe.
You gave even when I could not receive.
You warmed me when I was cold.
When I was timid you were bold.

Thank you my love for standing tall,
When I was afraid to fall.
Thank you for holding me tight
When I was paralyzed with fright.

Thank you for reflecting the love
Of our heavenly father up above.

My Husband, My Love, My Hero

Lord, you have assigned me my portion and my cup; you have made my lot secure. The boundary lines have fallen for me in pleasant places; surely I have a delightful inheritance. I will praise the Lord, who counsels me; even at night my heart instructs me. I have set the Lord always before me. Because he is at my right hand, I will not be shaken. Therefore my heart is glad and my tongue rejoices; my body will rest secure, because you will not abandon me to the grave, nor will you let your Holy One see decay. You have made known to me the path of life; you will fill me with joy in your presence, with eternal pleasures at your right hand.

Psalms 16:5-11

My husband Greg was born in 1968 to Kittie Ann and James Harry Tipton. He came into the world much the same way other children enter the world. Nothing special about his mother's pregnancy or the birth. What followed was nothing short of a miracle. After Greg's birth he was diagnosed with Spina-Bifida or Open Spine. This spinal defect was quite devastating during that time period because not a lot was known about it and treatment methods were scarce. In addition to lack of knowledge there was also a lack of technology. Greg's parents were given no great words of encouragement. They were told to expect the worst. Greg developed what they believed to be pressure on his brain and a procedure was scheduled for the following day. Kittie was told that maybe it was better to let her son go and be with Jesus and that he probably wouldn't have a quality life anyway.

Kittie began to pray constantly that God would spare Greg's life. She knew that God had a purpose and a plan for her son and she wanted to see him live to walk it out. God heard those prayers and the pressure disappeared leaving no need for the surgery. From that day on she encouraged her son to work at overcoming his disability. Always she reminded him that he was a precious gift to her and to the world.

Greg's dad, Harry stood beside him throughout the years in his own ways. He never missed a surgery spending the first night after each surgery in the hospital with Greg. This was important to Greg because a surgery during that time required admittance the night before surgery and hospital stays were longer.

Many of his surgeries took place out of state which required much sacrifice on their family. Greg is sure that at times his brother Chris felt left behind. No matter how difficult the challenge his family was committed to supporting him and helping him accomplish his goals.

I saw my husband for the first time in middle school. I knew the moment I looked at him that somehow our lives were to be intertwined. I did not actually meet Greg until we got to high school. I knew then that this was the man God had chosen for me.

As most teenagers we both had our ideas of what our lives would be like. As it turns out, we really did not have a clue. Greg went on to college and I married a man whom I had nothing in common with. Greg and I remained friends and were always a part of each others lives.

On June 29, 1988 I was blessed with the birth of my daughter Elizabeth Hope. Greg came to the hospital and waited with my brothers to congratulate me and my husband on her birth. Little did we know that life's journey would tie us together in much bigger ways.

Eventually my husband and I divorced due to his drinking and abusive behavior. Life was very confusing at that time. I had a young daughter and was trying to make a life for us. I do not know how we would have made it without family and friends. Greg and I stayed close and eventually he decided to go to Oklahoma and attend school to become an Air Traffic Controller.

We were both a little sad that he would be leaving. He told me that he did not want to be friends anymore. He wanted to marry me and have a family with me and Elizabeth. I was not inclined to want that. I knew what marriage was like, well at least I knew what I had been through. Greg left to go to school and I stayed in

Tennessee with my daughter. We talked every day on the phone and ran up horrendous phone bills. After about a month I started to realize what a huge void was in my life since he had left. I called Greg and told him that I needed him in my life. I put all my things in storage, flew to Oklahoma and we were married in a small wedding chapel.

I will never forget that day. I was so excited but also very scared. That was seventeen years ago and I can not believe all that God has done in our lives. It is amazing to me that while we tried to mess up our lives and did not listen to His will for our lives He was working to bring us together.

Seventeen years of love, honor and respect from my best friend. What more could a girl ask for? I look back and I realize that even when we tried to take the wheel and go down roads that God never meant for us to take, He watched over us. When we were willing to turn that wheel over to the Lord the journey took us where we needed to be.

Thirty nine years ago Greg's parents listened to what God spoke to their hearts. Because they chose the right road I have my husband and my children have their father. Greg has told me He believes that God used his disability to equip him for the ministry we have with our family.

I know that I am blessed daily by his presence in my life. I love and respect him, not because he demands it but because he leads our home with love. I cherish every moment I have had with him. Every memory is a special treasure. Our love has only grown stronger in the face of adversity.

I will not pretend that life has been easy for either of us. Greg has had numerous surgeries in his life. He walked despite what doctors said. He has had to face deteriorating hips and shoulders. He is currently in a wheelchair due to the loss of one shoulder. Greg continues to lead a full and happy life despite the challenges.

Every day presents new obstacles. Along with those obstacles come periods of depression, fear and uncertainty. Daily Greg looks to God for encouragement and strength. He continually emerges from conflict stronger and more excited about his walk with God. He goes to work each day with a positive attitude.

I know that every life he touches is changed forever. I know this because mine has been impacted most of all.

Marriage is difficult under the most perfect circumstances. We have faced issue that most couples will not face in a lifetime. Some health related, some relational. But with God as our foundation we have risen above those difficulties and are more in love than ever. I would never have realized as a silly girl of sixteen what God would do in our lives. I am so glad that God is in control.

Elizabeth

Watching you grow and mature steals my breath
My beautiful, sweet Elizabeth.
Tall and slender full of grace
Always wearing a smile upon your face.

Your beautiful brown eyes
Twinkle like the stars in the sky.
Full of humor and compassion
Always the model of elite fashion.

Laughing, smiling, playing pranks
Provoking in me a need to give thanks.
You open your mouth and let your voice ring
As praises to our God you sing.

I love you for the beautiful person you are Beth.
I will thank my God for you even unto death.
I am watching and waiting everyday
For what God has for you along the way.

So keep laughing at life
to chase away the strife.
Keep singing your song
as you skip along.

Journey through life with a hope that is true.
God will bless and always keep you.
I love you my angel sent from above
And I have learned the greatest of these is LOVE.

Songs of the Heart

> I will praise you O Lord with all my heart; I will tell of
> all your wonders. I will be glad and rejoice in you; I will
> sing praise to your name, O Most High.

> Psalms 9:1-2

Beth is our oldest child. She is a beautiful young woman with a song in her heart. The day I held her for the first time and touched her tiny fingers I knew she was special. I knew that God had an amazing plan for her life. Elizabeth means consecrated to God. I did not know that when I chose it. That name was important because her grandmother and great-grandmother both shared it.

Little did I know that I had given her such an important name. Nor did I realize how that meaning would impact her life.

Beth has always loved to sing. I think she came out singing. Everywhere she goes she is listening for music. A song is forever in her heart. I can recount many times over the years when I sat watching her as she played. She would sing to her dolls, the trees, sometimes just to herself. Her friends would be recruited into amateur concerts or skits with Beth as the director.

At the age of eleven she began writing her first song. The lyrics were beautiful and gave us all a glimpse into her heart. I knew as I read those words and listened to her sing them that she had a compassion for others and insight that most adults don't have.

She began to show an interest in missions and participated in youth mission trips. Imagine my agony when she asked to take a mission trip to Chili for two weeks over her birthday.

I had rarely been away from her for longer than a weekend. I could not hold her back. I placed her in God's hands and helped her pack. She came back so excited about the people there and all the work that had been accomplished. She grieved over leaving the friends she made and vowed to return someday. From that time on she revealed her heart for people more openly. She has always been a people person and loves to bring help and joy to those around her. At thirteen she recorded an album called Alone With God. I listen to the beautiful voice of my daughter and I feel only praise for my savior.

I am sure that growing up with so many disabled siblings has been difficult for her. She does not say this, but I am sure. There have been times the signs of jealousy, fatigue and frustration have been evident. She has worked alongside us and cared for these children through the years. She is a constant in their lives and ours. Daily her heart is revealed in her love and compassion for others.

She is grown now and my beautiful girl with a song in her heart will be starting to plan her own life soon. I do not know which path she will choose to do this. What I do know is that she will be wonderful at whatever she chooses.

I watch as she continues to grow in beauty and grace. She has now established a project called REACH. She uses her God given talent to raise money for small non-profit organizations by organizing a concert yearly. I wonder at the organizational skills of my once messy teenager. I stand amazed as I see the faces and hear the silence that comes when she opens her mouth to sing. She does not realize the impact her voice has on those around her.

Although Beth struggles daily with depression and a Bi-Polar disorder she gives everything to living life to the fullest. I know that God is helping her as I can hear it in her voice and see it in her smile.

I pray daily for this beautiful child and the struggles she experiences. I watch her cycle in and out of happiness and feel so helpless that I cannot change things for her. I watch her grow and become dependent on God and I know He is watching over her.

She probably does not recognize the encouraging balm her songs bring to those who are hurting and lost. I pray she will never lose the beautiful song in her heart. I pray that as she continues to grow into womanhood, she will allow God to work through her in the lives of others.

Her voice has been a life raft of encouragement on the stormy seas of our ministry. She is my hope and my comfort, and a joy to all who know her. My prayer for her is that God will give her strength to press on through each trial and come out on the other side stronger. I can only trust that she can feel or love and devotion to her and to our Lord. My hope is that she will continue to grow into a strong, fearless, and compassionate young woman who has endless boundaries in the Lord.

Suzanna

Suzanna brave and strong
with a determination that will never steer you wrong,
Everything seems so hard for you
but you try with all your might in everything you do.

Diligently seeking God daily in prayer
I look at you and see His face there.
Miracles, miracles in your little life
Only joy and thanks where they said there would be strife.

I used to cry at night for all I thought you had lost.
Then I realized that you were a fighter at all cost.
When they said you would never take a step
you charged your spirit and gathered your pep

When they told us you were blind
you opened your eyes wide, a new world to find.
Doctors told us words would never come
You would never say your name.
But God untied your tongue and your communication came.

Suzanna, my brave warrior maid
You came into our lives and there you stayed.
No matter what those doctors said
God changed the plans and took away the dread.

Remember always to look to God above
and you will be surrounded by overwhelming love.
A love so great and so true
enabling you in all you do.

A love so deep and so wide
you never feel empty inside.
Amazing grace so sweet the sound
that turned your little life around.

Faithful Warrior

For I know the plans I have for you," declares the Lord, "plans to prosper you and not to harm you, plans to give you hope and a future. Then you will call upon me and come and pray to me, and I will listen to you. You will seek me and find me when you seek me with your whole heart. I will be found by you," declares the Lord.

Jeremiah 29:11-13

When our sweet Suzanna entered this world thirteen weeks early she was not breathing. She experienced several strokes during her birth process that kept her hospitalized several months. She was not breathing and was resuscitated. For months she required a respirator to aid in breathing. She spent three months in the NICU. My daughter has been a faithful fighter from the beginning. Every challenge put before her she has found a way to conquer.

Suzanna's birth mom was only seventeen when she gave birth to a severely medically fragile infant. I am sure she was terrified to think of all that was ahead of her. I am told that her family stood by her and that they offered her support regardless of her choice.

I know that young woman was raised in church and I am sure that she struggled with guilt over breaking her vows to God. I believe it was her heart's desire to raise her daughter herself. But I also believe that thought was overwhelming to a seventeen year old.

After what I imagine was much struggle she made the choice to choose a family for her daughter. She felt that Suzanna would be better off with a family that could provide her with the best medical care possible. Her only request of us was to keep her involved in church. I am convinced that God spoke to her heart and allowed her to see God's plan for her daughter's life.

We first met Suzanna when she was six months old and ready to come home. The agency we went through asked that we meet her doctors and speak with her neurologist to get a clear picture of what we would be saying yes to. We were told that our little girl would never walk, talk, brush her own hair or communicate with us. We were told that we should walk away from this one and wait for the next baby. All the medical issues were overwhelming. Her heart beat was irregular, her breathing needed monitored twenty four hours a day. Keeping her at a healthy weight was nearly impossible while dealing with reflux. Then the most devastating news that so much of her brain was damaged that she would be severely mentally retarded and probably would not live through that first year with us. Well she made it alright. She is now a beautiful thirteen year old young woman of God.

From the first time I looked into her eyes I knew God had an amazing plan for her life. He spared her because she had a job to do for Him. Almost from the beginning we knew that life would be interesting with this little girl. From teaching her how to suck a bottle to the day she officially became a woman she has demonstrated an amazing determination to do all things BIG.

We struggled for many years with medical equipment, procedures, surgeries and therapies. Our first several years were a whirlwind of wires, medications, equipment and the advice of specialists. There were many times when we weren't sure if she would make it. There were times when we begged God for her life, for His mercy on her and us. I refused to believe the worst. Why would God let her live if it would all be a battle? God had an amazing plan, we just had to wait it out.

Suzanna has always been a mission minded girl. She puts the needs of others before her own. I find this difficult at times because I see her needs and her heart for others. I try not to hold her back from her calling. She told me when she was five that she really wanted to be a missionary. She did not know how that would work since she was in a wheelchair. Her idea of being a missionary was of someone who went into third world countries to preach the gospel and feed the hungry. Little did she know that God's idea of a missionary was a lot broader than hers.

She was always the one who donated her toys at Christmas time, brought home three shoe boxes to fill. She grew her hair out long so that she could donate it to be made into wigs for children going through cancer treatment.

Every day she has amazed us with her selfless acts of love toward others. It is awesome to see God work through her as she touched peoples lives.

When Suzanna was nine years old she came to us with a plan to open an equipment loan closet, where used medical and therapy equipment could be loaned out to people who needed them The idea arose from her own need for equipment. Suzanna has been in a wheelchair all of her life and requires adaptive equipment for every thing she does.

There have been many times that we needed equipment but had to wait extremely long periods of time. Sometimes when we would get this equipment it would not be the right size or her positioning needs had already changed. This was very frustrating to all of us. We also had several items that had been outgrown and needed a new home.

Suzanna felt God calling her to minister in this way to her community. She filled out grant proposals, applications and other types of paperwork. Before we knew it Suzie' Closet was in full operation. Our community responded in an amazing way. Equipment is donated to her on a regular basis and she has loaned items to many families over the past four years.

This little ministry has grown to offer financial assistance to families who must travel outside of their home area to receive medical treatment. She also coordinates volunteer groups, and resources to build ramps for individuals in wheelchairs. All this she does from her own chair.

In 2004 she was nominated for The Alexandra Scott Butterfly Award through the Volvo Corporation and received twenty-five thousand dollars from Volvo in 2005. That money she put to use by building a warehouse for all the equipment. Just as we have watched her grow into a beautiful caring young woman we have also had the tremendous blessing of watching her ministry grow.

I love her so much and feel such joy at all that she has allowed the Lord to accomplish through her little life. She lives life to the fullest, always taking great leaps of faith. I am amazed at the was she goes forward with no doubts. If only we could all have that faith.

As I have watched her grow I look on in amazement. I feel ashamed at times that I do not have the faith to do all that God places on my heart. I learn important life lessons from her every day.

My prayer is that she will never lose that blind faith and the love she has for the Lord and for others. She is twelve years old now and has exceeded her life expectancy, accomplished what the doctor's said would be impossible for her, and has captured our hearts fully. I see that God is blessing her richly and using her for His glory.

I am astounded that she has come so far. I think back to all the close calls, all the times we have prayed for her life. God chose to not only give her life but life more abundantly than we could imagine.

She has such zest for life I watch her teeter back and forth between the grown up business of running a non profit ministry and the joys and perils of preteen life. I often contemplate those first few moments of our lives together and I am at a loss for words. All of the fear and insecurity of those first moments fall away and leave me feeling blessed to be a part of all that God is doing.

I know that a time will come when I must let her go and find her own way. I feel confident that she will and can do it. I know when that time comes I will need much time with God to allay my fears and allow Him to keep me from foiling His plans. He certainly knew the plans He had for her, plans of hope and a future.

What started out to others as an insignificant life with no purpose, no hope of survival, God turned to value, love and determination. Suzanna is a gift to this world. God placed her in our midst as an example of His commandment to "Love one Another". May we all strive for that in hopes of glorifying Him.

Evan Tried and True

Evan is tried and Evan is true.
Evan is playing peek-a-boo.
Looking high and looking low
Searching for something
Only he knows.

The words are hard and will not come.
This may seem strange to some.
But Evan needs no words to say
The love he feels in so many ways.

Love that is deep and honest and true,
Love that radiates out to you.
Evan's faith is unfaltering and pure.
His pace is steady but it is sure.

Evan is steadfast, a soldier in God's army
Marching on and standing firm against the enemy.
Evan is tried and Evan is true.
Evan is playing peek-a-boo.

Our Silent Warrior

As for God, his way is perfect; the word of the Lord is flawless. He is a shield for all who take refuge in him. For who is God besides the Lord? And who is the Rock except our God? It is God who arms me with strength and makes my way perfect. He makes my feet like the feet of a deer; he enables me to stand on the heights. He trains my hands for battle; my arms can bend a bow of bronze. You give me your shield of victory, and your right hand sustains me; you stoop down to make me great. You broaden the path beneath me, so that my ankles do not turn.

Psalm 18:30-36

In February of 1997 we were blessed with Evan. What an amazing time in our lives. Little did we know that our faith was once more going to be challenged. We were excited at being chosen by Evan's birth mother as his future family. We met with the social worker with great anticipation.

I remember sitting there listening to our social worker as she told us of our son's history. We learned that his biological mother was only 15 when she gave birth to him. The identity of his father was unknown. I cannot imagine the fear his birth mom must have felt as she tried to tell her parents. I know those months of waiting the arrival of her baby must have been the most confusing of her life. I am confident that she struggle with conflicting emotions of keeping her baby or giving him up for adoption. She was probably surprised and a little frightened when he was delivered 5 weeks early by cesarian section. I can imagine her holding him in her arms and looking deep into her heart for the right answer.

The first time the pediatrician looked at Evan he knew something was not right. He knew just from looking at him that our son had a genetic abnormality.

A genetic specialist was called in and tests performed. It was confirmed. Our son has Prader-Willi Syndrome. This syndrome's classic symptoms included moderate to severe mental retardation, severe tantrums and behaviors, an insatiable hunger and various medical problems resulting from the inevitable obesity.

That diagnosis was, I am certain, a devastating blow. His birth mom had to be overwhelmed. To have a baby at fifteen was overwhelming enough. To be told that your baby has a genetic disorder must have been extremely frightening.

I am sure that after much prayer and soul searching she came to a heartbreaking decision. She made the mature decision to give Evan up for adoption. I will forever feel indebted to this brave young woman. She has a special place in my heart and in our family.

Without her brave choice I would not have my son. She has given us a wonderful gift. A rare treasure that is beyond compare.

Our social worker advised us of Evan's needs and his diagnosis. As I listened to what we would face I was overwhelmed. Did this birth mom make the right choice in us? Would we be what he needed? Suddenly I was terrified. I could handle the medical issues, but things like eating out of the trash, running away and tantrums? Was I prepared for this? Everything seemed so grim for him and hopeless to us.

We did not make a decision that day. We asked our social worker for time to pray about it and discuss it as a family. I struggled with whether or not we were equipped to handle his needs. Were we the right parents for him? How would we keep him from hurting himself or eating himself to death?

We were praying hard for an answer. We were afraid but felt certain that God would not place this child before us if He did not have a plan. Once again our faith was being challenged. After much prayer, and discussion the answer came to us. We had only to listen. We stepped out on faith once more.

There are daily struggles living with Evan but the rewards are so great_ We help Evan fight the battle of an endless hunger. He fights to get his thoughts and words to connect. Evan has very little language he can use. It is hard for him to communicate so most of the time he fights this war in silence.

I hold Evan close to me and assure him that he is stronger than this syndrome. Every day he is learning more and more about how to cope. We have set healthy boundaries and given him a solid routine. Evan is communicating in his own way. He does not have mental retardation but he does struggle with a learning disability.

Every day is a battle for food. In spite of the fact that every where we go he is constantly seeking out food he is not even overweight. He wants to learn, to exercise, and to be in control of his life. I am proud of his determination. He has a love for God that warms my soul.

I watch him as he fills out his prayer card at church asking prayer for those he loves. How humbling it is to see him struggle daily, but take the time to pray for others. I watch him grow and I am amazed at God's protection over his little life.

I was not surprised at all to find the meaning of his name to be "Jehovah has found favor". I see God's favor every day on Evan's life. As he grows I see a glimpse of the man he will become I see his need for independence coming to fruition. I become aware of the fact that one day I will have to let go. The struggle within my heart amazes me. The fact that God has grown a love so deep where there was fear and suspicion. The irony that I will someday be asked to let go of the very thing I was unsure I needed or wanted does not escape me.

I thank God every day for bringing Evan into our lives to teach us humility, bravery and endurance. Every day that he wins this battle is a day closer to winning the war that rages inside him. I am blessed to be Evan's mother. I am grateful for his biological mother's decision to choose us. There has not been one moment of regret that Evan came into our lives. But most of all I am amazed to watch my silent warrior fight this battle successfully with God's help.

I wander at times why it is so hard to walk out into God's plan. My prayer is that I will continue to learn through my son to be brave and face challenges head on. I have learned that we do not always have the knowledge of what we need or what is best for us.

Daily as I watch my son grow into a young man I am reminded that God's will for our lives is so divinely connected with the lives of others. I am equally astounded at the strength I see reflected in Evan's eyes. Supernatural strength, the kind that can only come from the Holy Spirit.

I can only pray that I can feel that strength as I walk this path with my children. Our family is blessed by Evan's presence. I want him to grow in confidence as he finds his place in this big world.

I pray for certainty in his heart that his family loves him, wants him and will stand by him. He is perfect in God's eyes. What our world calls defective or Savior calls usable. I know that He will use Evan for big things. He has already used him in amazing ways in his mommy's life.

Katie

Katie bright and beautiful with smiling eyes of blue
You make it easy for one to be dutiful in doing
all that's required in caring for you.
You look at me with dancing eyes and laughter in your voice,
Telling my heart to ignore all the lies and that
loving you is not a burden but a choice.

Thank you darling in so many ways for all the joy you bring.
Thanks for the laughter and the love that fills my
day, the song that my heart now sings.
Katie bright and beautiful with smiling eyes of blue,
You make it easy for me to be dutiful in doing
all that's required in loving you.

Katie's eyes so bright and shiny, a beautiful shade of blue.
Katie's eyes so full of joy that it reaches the heart of you.
Katie's eyes dreaming dreams so grand they inspire you to do your best.
Katie's eyes so deep in thought that you can only guess what
wonders lie in wait within life's awkward mess.

Katie's eyes searching for the hows and whys
Always uncovering the peace that within you lies.
Katie's eyes so full of faith and love
Keep you feeling eternally close to God above.

Katie's Smile

I praise you because I am fearfully and wonderfully made; your works are wonderful, I know that full well. My frame was not hidden from you when I was made in the secret place. When I was woven together in the depths of the earth, your eyes saw my unformed body. All the days ordained for me were written in your book before one of them came to be.

Psalms 139:14-16

When I remember back to when Katie was born I am amazed at how God worked. We were not even trying to adopt at the time. Our social worker had called inquiring as to if we might know of a family who would be equipped to handle her medical needs. Katie was born twelve weeks early and had fluid on her brain. Her life was very fragile.

My husband knew immediately that this was to be our child. God spoke to his heart right then. We discovered that Katie had been a planned pregnancy. Her biological parents discovered through an ultra sound early in the pregnancy that she had fluid around her brain. They were given information about a surgery that could be done and told that she could possibly experience some degree of brain damage. I am certain that they were terrified by the enormity of how this would change their lives. They were probably terrified at the prospect of trying to raise a baby with medical issues. I am sure they questioned what her quality of life would. I wanted to believe that they agonized over their choices before making the decision to abort the pregnancy.

God had a different plan. Katie's biological mom developed a condition called Placenta-Privia and Our daughter was delivered by C-Section twelve weeks early. God treasured her little life and had plans for her. She came kicking and screaming into our lives at three months of age after an extended hospital stay. I knew from the moment I held her that she was meant to be my daughter. I was saddened to find out that her birth parents did not want any contact with her. They wanted no progress reports on her condition. They simply wanted to forget she happened.

I have experienced many emotions over their decision. Obviously I am incredible happy and feel blessed that she is part of our family. I have to admit that at times I am sad and angry at their absolute abandonment of her. I struggle not to judge them too harshly. I feel that in some way they felt they were protecting her and acted out of some sense of compassion.

As we watched her grow that first few years we were amazed at what a beautiful and smart girl she grew into. She had the most amazing blue eyes and gorgeous blonde hair. Her smile was and is infectious. At the age of two the shunt that had been surgically placed to control the pressure of fluid on her brain malfunctioned. For the first time in that two years I was afraid she would not make it.

Katie was hospitalized and had to be airlifted to Carolina's Medical Center for an emergency shunt revision. Suddenly her little life was in the balance. I found myself on my face before God, begging for her healing and her life. After hours of surgery she was placed in the pediatric intensive care unit. I will never forget that tedious wait. I prayed with all my heart. I cried because I longed to see the smile that had been absent for days.

The joy that filled my heart when the nurses called us back to the unit. "She wants her mommy," they said. What wonderful words! As I sat there rocking her in the chair beside her bed and peered down at her sweet face I was reminded once again of the protection that we receive under God's wing. As she looked up at me with sleepy eyes her smile emerged, a reminder of God's covenant with us. His promise to hear our prayers and to comfort and protect us. He will never leave us or forsake us. Katie's smile is like a rainbow, bright with the promise of a future and hope.

Now she is eight years old. We have been six years with no further shunt problems. She is walking in her walker and uses a wheelchair. We have recently been told by Katie's neurosurgeon that she may have outgrown the need for her shunt. Yet another miracle.

Few things have changed about Katie in all these years. She is a happy, beautiful, blue eyed cherub. She is full of life and lives it to the fullest. She never forgets that a day is full of amazing opportunities and that she must go at them with all of her might. Katie cherishes her family and does not let a day go by without telling us so.

It was devastating to me when my daughter asked me for the first time, "Did my birth parents love me?" How does a mother answer that question honestly and still protect her from feeling rejected. I can remember holding that precious little girl in my lap and explaining how afraid her biological parents must have felt. I shared with her that God saw the beauty in her little life and shared how He had stretched out his hands to save her and give her a family and a future full of hope and joy.

With tearful eyes she looked up at me and said that she would praise God every day for our family. Katie wrote a beautiful letter to her birth parent telling them that she loved them and forgave them for thinking of taking her life. She thanked them for their later decision to allow her to be adopted, saying she was happy with her family and loved them very much. My beautiful daughter has taught me so much about forgiveness and redemption.

Katie faces every challenge with a smile and a giggle. She has taught us how fragile and precious life really is. She daily gives us the courage to face every obstacle with a smile. Katie's smile, so bright and beautiful is our rainbow. Our symbol of promises made and promises kept. I thank God daily for the honor of knowing her and sharing my life with her. I thank Him for the constant reminder that He is watching over us, protecting us and has a plan for our lives.

My prayer is that Katie will know what a precious treasure she is to us all. The world may see her as imperfect or defective, but God sees her as fearfully and wonderfully made. He looks on her with joy. Katie's beauty radiates from within. It is the beauty of God's providence in her little life.

My prayer is that as she grows she will continue to know the unconditional and undying love of her Heavenly Father.

Janet

I look into your beautiful face
and I know that God is in this place.
I brush my finger across your cheek
and I can hear His voice speak.

I watch you smile and I know
that you are never alone.
I know that God has put us together at last
to heal the wounds of a time past.

I am sure for you it is hard to trust
but this we will learn for we must
Because this love is real and right
of that sweetheart, we must never lose sight.

So come and be with us
let us love you and teach you to trust.
Let me hold you, hug you and play.
Let us allow our love to grow day by day.

Let every touch bring a smile.
Let every inch of progress grow into a mile.
Together we can do AMAZING things
as we explore the new joy that each day brings.

You grow in our hearts minute by minute.
We cannot imagine our life without you in it.

So my quiet angel tucked away inside
trust this love and know you have tried.

God can heal ALL hurts and pains
and help us learn to love again.
Janet, don't slip away and hide.
Don't lock yourself away inside.

Come out among us and be brave.
We all love you and you are safe.
Jesus loves you! Yes he does.
No matter what happens He still loves.

Let go of the past hurt and pains.
Let God break loose those binding chains.
Daughter of my heart daily I plead,
that through me God will plant a seed.
A seed of love to reflect God's grace.
A seed of joy to put a smile upon your face.
A seed of hope that you may seek the future.
A seed of faith that you may be nurtured.
A seed of compassion that you my learn to love.
A seed of grace that you may seek God above.

You may not be bone of my bone
or flesh of my flesh.
But you are the child of my heart
and because of you I am truly blessed.

Tears From the Heart

But I am like an olive tree flourishing in the house of God; I trust in God's unfailing love for ever and ever. I will praise you forever for what you have done; in your name I will hope, for your name is good. I will praise you in the presence of your saints.

Psalms 52:8-9

It never fails to amaze me what miracles lie in the everyday experiences of life. This is the story of how very ordinary children affected my life in an extraordinary way. My husband Greg and I have been married seventeen wonderful years and we have built a unique family together. We have six terrific children. All but our oldest are adopted and have various special needs.

When we started our life together, I don't think either of us realized the path God would lead us to travel. All of our journeys with our children are unique and wonderful. But our lives were forever changed when God asked the impossible and then showed us the possibilities.

In September of 2003 God blessed us with an angel daughter. Janet was a beautiful child who captured our hearts from the first moment we laid eyes on her. Her small stature and long beautiful brown hair that almost reached the back of her knees drew you to gaze into her amazing green eyes. Those eyes will forever hold my heart. Janet could not talk, but those eyes communicated every fear, every happy thought, every giggle and all the love she felt in her heart for those around her.

We met Janet in September and knew that although there would be problems we wanted her in our family. We looked into her eyes and knew that no matter what lie ahead we were meant to be together. None of us had any way to know the enormity of what we would face as a family, or what our precious daughter would face in the year following her homecoming.

This is the story of an amazing little girl who faced adversity her entire life and left a legacy that will remain forever in the hearts of all who knew her. This is also the story of the lives she touched and the lessons she taught us. I will attempt to tell our story as honestly as I possible can. Regarding the facts about the beginning of her life, I have only records given to us about the DSS investigation and their relationship with her family. I will write from my heart and give you the facts as I know them to be.

I only hope that her story will touch you and leave you with a stronger faith, a stronger zeal for life, and the ability to love a little deeper. My prayer is that, as you get to know Janet and our family you will examine your own life and learn more about our creator as she teaches you to seek the purpose you were created for.

I also pray that you will see our Savior's providence in your own life as you watch God work in her life to provide a family for her where there was none. May you feel God's peace as you walk through our difficult journey and experience our ups and downs. Last but not least I pray that in some way God will reveal his unconditional love for you in a new and amazing way as you see the last year of our life with Janet unfold and God's plans come to completion in her life.

Janet Marie was born on December 6, 1996 to Beverly and Billy. Her birth was like any other birth, uneventful in its simplicity. She came into the world kicking and screaming like any other tiny morsel of humanity angry at suddenly being transplanted from the safety of the quiet, dark womb in which she grew to a noisy, busy place full of light and strange voices. I am sure she experienced great relief when placed within the safe confines of her birth mother's arms. I feel that she was probably in awe at the sight of a face to match the voice and heartbeat she had come to recognize as her mother.

As she adjusted to her new environment I am sure that Beverly had many thoughts as she took in every speck of Janet's being. I am sure she counted every finger and every toe. I am equally convinced that dreams of a beautiful future for her child passed through her mind as she ran her fingers through the shock of dark brown hair and gazed into Janet's eyes.

I do not know if Janet's mother could have known that their future would be precarious. I believe that she adored the bundle in her arms. I feel she set out to care for her and love her as any mother does. I don't know if this is truth or not. Maybe it is a lie I tell myself to keep the hurt at bay. Since I have no knowledge of the woman's true nature, I choose to see her as a loving mother who wanted Janet and loved her.

Janet was a healthy baby and left the hospital with her mother to begin life with her family. I believe that she was rocked, held and fed with love. There were photos taken and hugs and kisses given. Janet began her life being adored.

But as life often does, reality set in. Billy worked long hours at a local factory. He was often gone at night leaving Beverly to care for Janet alone. They coped with life as it happened. Two O'clock feedings and diaper changes, burping and the middle of the night play times became daily rituals. Janet's mother began to feel lonely and frustrated. She was tired and needed to rest.

Then as if things weren't bad enough, Janet became ill. She was running a fever and throwing up. Beverly called the pediatrician, and tried to do everything he advised, but nothing was working. Then the crying started. She paced with Janet, she rocked her, tried to feed her, and when those things didn't work she tried changing her, laying her down and singing to her.

Finally after many attempts to calm her, she may have placed the baby in bed with her, desperately hoping for sleep to find them both. Things only went from bad to worse. Then on February 1, 1997, in a moment of desperation something happened that would forever change their lives and the lives of many of others along the way.

The young mother shook her baby out of frustration. Janet apparently stopped breathing as a result. She was taken to the doctor. When she arrived at the pediatricians office, she was greyed in color and extremely lethargic. After admitting her to the hospital the doctor became suspicious that her illness was the result of a brain injury. Tests were order to further investigate the problem. A CAT Scan revealed a severe brain injury that was believed to be caused by asphyxiation.

The doctors talked to Janet's mother and father. I am told that Beverly kept a non responsive attitude even after hearing that her child would most likely die before the night was over. This also alarmed the physician treating Janet and the decision was made to contact the authorities.

DSS became involved. After talking to both parents separately and confirming information given to them about each parent's whereabouts DSS felt that Beverly was the one who had abused Janet. Her mother and father inevitably separated. Each one struggled with emotional pain over what had happened. Janet's mother was probably in shock over what she had done, and her father surely struggled with the enormity of it all. Both struggled with what would happen over the next days and weeks. The doctors gave little hope that Janet would survive through the night.

Janet fought for every breath and heartbeat. She did survive through the night. Janet remained at Wake Forrest University Baptist Hospital until February 20, 1997. She was given a poor prognosis of severe mental retardation, respiratory problems, and a shortened life span. On February 20, 1997, DSS had secured custody of Janet. It was determined that the best place for Janet was in a care facility. She was admitted to Amos Cottage as a temporary placement with hopes of reunification with her family. While Janet was residing at Amos Cottage, she was reevaluated frequently to judge improvement. Medical issues were dealt with and treatment put into place. Janet lived at Amos Cottage until April 16, 1997. During that time Janet received all types of therapy, nutritional assessments, and the medical care necessary. On April 16, 1997, Janet was able to leave Amos Cottage and was placed into the first of many foster homes. There she was cared for and loved. She began to stabilize and thrive. But it was not to last. By June 2, 1997, Janet was readmitted to Amos Cottage. Little did anyone know that this would become a trend in Janet's little life. The staff at Amos Cottage worked hard to keep Janet's situation stable and give her good medical care. There she received all the care she needed. She had everything but the love of a family.

The search was on for another foster family. The plan was to give Janet stability and allow her to be cared for by a family. On June 18, 1997, Janet was placed in yet another foster family. They were taught to care for her various medical needs and given support in hopes of creating a safe, loving environment for Janet. After a short time she became ill and was admitted to the hospital for five days. When she had recovered, she returned to her foster home. She remained there until September 18, 1997 when she was moved to a Child Care Ministry foster home where she remained until November29, 1997. How horrible that a baby should have to endure such constant upheaval_ She must have been so confused.

I am told that Janet's birth father made every effort to do all that DSS asked him to do to get her back. On November 29, 1997, Janet was placed back in the custody of her father. I often wonder if she recognized his voice, or remembered the feel of his arms as he held her. It would seem that things were finally coming together for Janet and that her life would settle into some normal routine.

Janet still required G-Tube feedings, 24 hours monitoring for seizures, medications and came home on a heart monitor. In addition to dealing with medical issues Janet still required the care that any infant would require. Her dad hired a home health professional to help care for Janet. Life continued to happen and as the reality sank in life became overwhelming for Billy. I am sure that Janet's father tried very hard to do what was right. I can only imagine the emotional roller coaster he rode daily. I know that when he looked into his little girls face the guilt and regret overwhelmed him. To be alone trying to raise a critically ill infant must have been tremendously difficult. Billy, who was an alcoholic soon sank to his all time low.

A call was placed to DSS The social worker and the police arrived at the house to find Billy passed out and a gun lying close to him. A complaint was made by the home health aide. The authorities woke him up and told Billy that they were removing Janet from the home. He began to assist in getting her things together. I imagine that although he felt the failure weighing heavy upon him there had to be a sense of relief. On November 20, 1998, Janet was placed in yet another foster care home.

By March 26, 1999, Janet was once again being moved. This time she was placed in a Specialized foster home. It was the hope of DSS that her needs could be better met by a family with special training in caring for children with special needs. She remained there a total of five days_ So much for trying to maintain stability. On April 1, 1999, she was moved again, this time to a foster care home outside of her county. Janet remained there until January 16, 2000. At that time a decision was made to place Janet in a long term care facility until an adoptive placement could be made. Janet remained at the Howell Center/Clear Creek until she was placed in our home on September 6, 2003. Things stabilize medically for Janet while in the care of Howell's Center. She had only one hospitalization while in their care. While Janet was doing well from a medical standpoint there were those, who still believed that she would be happier in a family environment. Janet may not have had a traditional family to love her, but there were those who loved her with all their hearts and hoped against all odds for a family for Janet. Janet received all of her therapies, schooling, medical care, and daily care from trained professionals.

I have no way of knowing how many people she came in contact with, but I would imagine the numbers were high. I certainly know that it made it hard for her to trust any one person. Daily she was bombarded with strangers. There were those who did not see Janet as a whole person with feelings. They went through the motions of caring for her daily needs sometimes never speaking to her, never hugging her or holding her. There were others who said good morning and good night, who called her by name and made her smile. To those people I am forever grateful for brightening her life. She was given birthday parties, Christmas presents and taken on outings. I don't know what Janet felt about being in a care facility, but I believe that by that time she was quite indifferent to the situation.

I don't think it really mattered to her who took care of her or even what they did to her. Janet had never remained in a family long enough to bond. Everyone was so busy just trying to meet medical needs that no one noticed that a little girl was getting lost. She became a case file, and a lot of big medical terms. She became a bed on the Blue wing of Howell's Center. Two very special people saw this happening and worked hard to keep Janet from falling through the cracks. Tawanna, Janet's DSS worker and Cynthia, the social worker for Howell's Center hoped beyond hope for a family. Tawanna used every avenue available to recruit an adoptive family for Janet while Cynthia gave her the extra attention and love she needed. Together, two women who were so different in many ways found common ground and made an amazing impact on Janet's life.

For the first time in a lot of years she was being loved and cared for on an emotional level. She was learning to give and receive love. I do not know if these two women know the important role they played in preparing her for a family. I do not know if they recognize the value of the gift they gave my daughter. I can only hope that they were able to receive the rare gift that Janet gave to them. Every smile she gave meant she trusted them and that they were important to her. Every coo, every joyful noise meant she trusted them enough to share her feelings with them. I thank these women for impacting my daughter's life, for seeing her when she was invisible to others. They chose to bring light to our little girl's dark existence. That is a gift to be treasured. I have tucked these things away in my heart where they will remain forever.

Suddenly Janet had hope where there was none. She had friends where only strangers were before. Her journey had been long and lonely, the paths filled with potholes and detours. The great thing about a journey is that many roads lead to the same destination. God was watching out for Janet and he had a plan. He had a plan for her future_ Plans that were for her best. Little did we know that those plans would include our family. We also did not know how those plans would forever impact out lives.

I am convinced that God brings a miracle into your life when you least expect it. Sometimes we can pray for a miracle and be discouraged by never seeing one. Yet other times they come at the most unexpected times and in the strangest forms. Ours came in the form of a beautiful angel with long brown hair and the most captivating smile. Janet came into our lives and blessed us greatly and in unexpected ways.

There are times when I look back and do not know how our family got through all that happened. There are times when I ask why. Then there are times when I just rest in the beauty of what God did within our family. I take a deep breath and stand in awe at the grace and glory of my Lord. God has a way of showing us that we have potential to do extraordinary things when we allow him to work through us.

When Greg and I began our journey together 18 years ago, we never imagined the things God would do in our lives. God constructed our family in a unique way and we have adopted six children. All of them have medical needs. The daily routine is quite often very strenuous both physically and emotionally. Our children are all wonderful. When our family decided to adopt again we had no idea, what God would call us to do. We knew that he had gifted us to be able to care for special needs' children so there was no question that we would adopt another child that was medically fragile.

Once we made our decision to adopt again, the search began. We began to pray that God would lead us to the child he had chosen for us. We began researching to find out what children were waiting to be adopted. We first saw Janet's photo and profile on an adoption website. We felt such a real connection. Feeling as if God had led us right to her, we contacted our social worker. After several weeks of waiting we called our social worker back and were told that there had been no response from Janet's case worker. She told us that it probably meant that Janet had already been adopted. What disappointment we felt. There had been such a connection. As we continued our search for the child God would provide for our family we continued to pray that wherever Janet was she would be blessed. We prayed for her to be well loved and cared for.

Imagine our surprise, when a year later at a conference for adoptive and foster care families we saw Janet's photo on display with other children that needed adoptive families_ We immediately contacted our social worker and again gave her the information. Within only a few weeks Janet's adoption case worker contacted us to set up a visit. We were so excited. We already knew in our hearts that Janet belonged with our family. We received a call from our social worker. She wanted to give us more updated information on Janet. We were told of her history of abuse and that she was profoundly mentally retarded and that we might want to reconsider because she would be very different from our children. The other issue was that she had been institutionalized. They were reluctant to place her with our family due to her level of care.

Greg and I prayed about it and felt God telling us to move forward. We told our social worker that we wanted to meet Janet and that we were committed to following through with the adoption if they chose us to be her family. A meeting was set up at the Howell Center. There we met with the medical staff and social workers. We also got to talk to Janet's teacher.

We were told that Janet was pretty non responsive most of the time. As they were bringing her in, we were told not to expect a lot of reaction.

I have written on my heart what took place next. As Janet was pushed through the doorway of that of that conference room, she looked first at me, then at my husband and stiffened her arms, turned her head and smiled. Her whole face lit up_ She knew exactly what was going on.

Throughout the remainder of our time there she continued to try to interact with us. By the time we were ready to leave everyone in the room was in tears. There was no doubt in our minds that Janet belonged with our family. I believe that everyone else felt it too. We left her there with aching hearts to await a decision from the adoption committee. Within a few weeks we had the answer. We had been chosen to be her family. We rejoiced and thanked God for this miracle.

Plans were made for frequent visits that would take place over the following month. Every week we would travel to Charlotte, North Carolina and visit. Soon our visits progressed into weekend visits in our home. Our other children loved to take her home with us. We began to prepare our home and our hearts to receive our new daughter. Each day we all fell more and more in love with Janet. It soon became very painful to leave her after each visit. We sent cards to her daily to fill the void and asked Cynthia to read them to her. Cynthia would call me and report Janet's reactions to the words we wrote from our heart. We were told that the staff often wanted to hear what we were writing to Janet. She had become a very special little girl to everyone in her life.

A placement day was set for September 6, 2003. Janet was coming home. Oh the joy that filled our hearts as we began to anticipate a lifetime with her. God had already started bringing changes in how she responded and interacted. We were so excited about the possibilities that lie ahead for her. The prayers of our family, friends and our church family were endless and much appreciated. The day that we brought Janet home was the beginning of an amazing journey.

We quickly settled into a routine. We had Janet evaluated by new doctors and therapists. Janet began receiving therapy and other services. Janet had almost no movement in her arms and legs. She could move her head well and had involuntary movement in her extremities. Every day I would massage her body and move her arms and legs through a series of range of motion exercises. With every movement prayers went up, and peace settled in my heart. God put peace and determination in my heart. Janet learned to eat food by mouth. She soon developed her own system for approving and disapproving what foods she wanted. Our oldest daughter Beth taught her to activate a toy with her head. She soon gained movement in her arms and began to kick her legs with purpose. God was working in her little life every day.

When Janet first came home, we saw a lot of distrust. She had her own way of shutting us out when she felt uncomfortable with us. She soon realized that we were there for good and that we could be trusted. She bonded well with everyone in our family. She and Evan developed an amazing bond. They understood each other. Maybe they were drawn together by their inability to communicate. I think they had their own way of communicating. We realized how strong that bond was when Evan would start walking toward Janet, saying _Evan here Jannie_ reaching her at the very moment a seizure would begin. Evan took time to talk to her and play with her even when others overlooked her. They had a very special relationship.

She learned to communicate her feelings. She would laugh and smile when she was happy. She would turn her head furiously left to right when she was upset. Janet also began to try to say words. This little girl could feel and communicate. We became excited at the possibilities she had. Suddenly her future looked much brighter. As a family we began to set goals. We worked hard at helping her meet her maximum potential.

Every day was filled with dreams for her future. Every new morning help hope for Janet to improve. Learning new skills took time, but that was something we could give her. Time seemed a small gift. Time is something that we all took for granted. Another minute, hour, day, or week. It seemed as if we had all the time in the world. Little did we know.

Two months after we brought Janet home she began to experience hypothermia. We would take her temperature only to find it very low. Her seizures seemed to be under control with the medication. We scheduled an appointment to take her to a pediatric neurologist in Greenville, SC. After doing a CT Scan of her brain the doctor told us that Janet's brain had apparently continued to die. She was functioning on brainstem activity only. He saw evidence of calcification on the brainstem also. This indicated that she was losing brainstem function also.

She was slowly dying. We were told that her hypothalamus gland was calcifying and that her body could not regulate her body temperature. The doctor also told us he was unsure of what was causing this condition. If we did not identify the reason her brain continued to die it could be fatal. We were told that one day she would just stop breathing on her own. There was nothing we could do. We were sent away with a terminal diagnosis and crushed dreams.

I grieved so much that day. I grieved for all that Janet and her family had lost. I grieved all the lost hopes and dreams we had for her future. More than anything I grieved for our family and the loss we would all feel. How could I tell my precious children that their beautiful sister was slipping away from us? How could I tell them that there was nothing to be done about it? I felt so helpless.

We returned home with heavy hearts. We talked with our pediatrician. He made a plan to treat her decreasing sodium levels and to try to locate the cause of this. Janet became ill and developed wheezing in her chest. We were referred to a pulmonologist. He treated her with antibiotics and sent us home with a cough assist machine. Janet was too weak to cough. Twice a day we had to use a machine to move the mucous trapped in her lungs. A sleep study revealed that she had apnea. She would often stop breathing for more than thirty seconds several time and hour. Lack of oxygen to the brain during these times was the cause of the continual dying of her brain.

We finally had the reason. But it was too late. The damage was permanent. An enormous amount of medical equipment invaded our home. Janet's bedroom quickly became mini hospital. We had to learn to operate several pieces of equipment. We settled into a daily routine of using the cough assist machine twice a day, adding respiratory medications, and putting on the apnea monitor to be worn through the day. I cannot tell you how difficult it is as a mother to become a nurse overnight.

We began to prepare our family for the inevitable. Some of our extended family could not accept the news. As people commonly do, some chose to stand by us, and others hid there heads in the sand. Friend and family members all reacted in there own way. I am sorry to say that most of them pulled away. I don't blame them or feel anger toward them. They did what they had to do to protect themselves. I feel very sad for Janet. She did not get to know all of them as well as she should have been allowed. They also missed out on the joy she could have brought to their hearts.

I must say that most of our friends and family offered their love, prayers and support. Our adoption agency and Janet's social worker backed us when we chose to follow through with our adoption. They gently gave us options, and wanted us to know that whatever we chose, they would stand behind us.

There were many times that we felt scared and alone. I have never prayed harder in my life. Suddenly every second held priority. Time was my enemy. No one could tell us when that final moment would come. Each new day was a treasure.

As time went on we discovered that life went on. Valentines Day came along with Janet's birthday, other birthdays, Christmas, and Mother's Day. I thank God every day for the blessing of sharing those times with her. Mother's day was different for me that year. I have no words to express the mixture of emotions I felt that day. I spent a lot of time just holding my children and realizing how fragile life really is. My regret is that my husband did not get to have a Father's Day to celebrate with her.

We watched as she slowly grew weaker. She soon needed oxygen twenty-four hours a day. She began sleeping more. Every day we got her out of bed, showered and dressed her. We refused to let a moment go by without her. She lost her ability to eat by mouth and we had to feed her only through her g-tube. Every day I moved her arms, legs and head, grieving her losses. Things had seemed to be going well. She had learned things that people said were impossible for her to learn.

We ran the race with our emotions. I went from praying, to pleading that somehow evolved into trying to make a deal with God. Nothing worked. When I finally exhausted all my strength, I broke down and cried my heart out. I asked God to forgive me and I gave it all to him. I prayed that he would give me peace in my heart where there was only panic. I prayed for strength when I felt so weak. I begged God to give me rest when I was scared to sleep. I asked him to somehow let me know when she needed me. I could be strong for her. I could do anything for my baby that He required.

The one thing I begged of God every day was that she would not be alone. All of her life she had basically been alone. I prayed with all my strength that God would not let her feel alone in this final season of her life.

Watching our daughter decline quickly was the most difficult thing we have had to do as a family. Daily she slipped further and further away from us. We had no option but to wait. Waiting for the last moment of one person's life is the most trying thing to do. We laughed, we cried, we prayed for miracles. We always had peace in our heart. We knew that whether God granted our miracle for Janet on this earth or in eternity she would be whole and happy.

Often I would go into Janet's room at night and lay beside her on her bed and hold her. I looked at her and wondered what she thought of us. She would wake up an smile her sweet smile at me and I saw only love in her eyes. I will never forget those eyes. Those eyes communicated so much to my heart about my little girl.

As Janet became weaker it was necessary to stay at home as much as possible. She could not go out for risk of infection. Our final weekend with her she was sick. We took her to the pulmonologist. He increased the frequency of the cough assist and asked us to suction Janet after each use. Her oxygen saturation was falling and he ordered another oxygen compressor to be brought in. By this time she was using a Bi-Pap Ventilator. The oxygen was hooked directly into the ventilator. I stayed up late with her. I sang to her, and prayed for her. Every breath was such a struggle. My prayer changed for Janet that night. I prayed only for her comfort and peace. I prayed that the oxygen would help make her comfortable.

At five O'clock in the morning I woke up feeling uneasy. I woke my husband and told him I was going to check on the children. When I entered Janet's room the monitor showed that her oxygen level was in the forties. I did the cough assist and tried to suction her. She clamped her mouth together and would not allow it. I began to panic. I went to my husband. Greg called the doctor. He told us that it was time and that we should call the ambulance. He was sure she did not have long.

We knew it was going to happen. We knew it was time, but we did not know how to let go. We woke our other children to say their good-byes and then settled them into our bed together. We went to her then. We held her and cried. Finally we silenced the alarm on the monitor. The monitor was flashing twenty-seven over and over again. Still she was holding on. Suddenly I realized, she didn't want to leave us any more than we wanted her to go.

She was holding on for us. I kissed her and told her that I loved her. I said to her "Janet I don't want to let you go, but if you see Jesus that means he wants you to go with him. If you see him you run baby. Mommy and Daddy will be okay." Then the most amazing thing happened. She opened her eyes, smiled peacefully, took a deep breath and was gone.

I would like to tell you that we gave up gracefully. But I for one cried. I will never be without this insatiable aching in my heart. But I felt God's spirit in that room that morning and I got the blessing of being allowed to be with her as she was ushered into the presence of God.

There were struggles in the months to follow. We all hurt. We all missed her. But God brought us out of the wilderness as a whole family. We were stronger, wiser and more aware of the awesomeness of our Savior. We each dealt with Janet's death in our own way. We each took away something special from our experience. For me Janet's death made my salvation more real. I no longer take for granted the sacrifice God made in giving us his Son. I know also the pain Mary felt in her heart as she watched her son beaten an suffering, dying on that cross.

I also know the joy that comes in the morning. The beauty of the memories, the blessings bestowed and the glory of our Savior. I thank God every day for the peace that grows in my heart and for the healing balm that every moment alone with him brings.

If you are experiencing grief and pain let his peace run over you, bathing you in comfort. Don't run from him, run straight into his arms. Weeping may remain for a night but Joy does come in the morning.

Cody

Cody with your eyes so bright
you bounced your way into my heart.
Into the darkness you brought light.
I knew I loved you from the start.

It was hard for you to learn to trust.
You were scared at first and tested
You would cry and fight all of us
When you realized you were truly loved you rested.

Your beautiful smile so full of love
and your laughter full of joy
are blessings from God above.
In the storms of life you are my buoy.

Your name means comfort and that you are.
You came into my life when my heart hurt.
Every day you teach me to look for love afar.
Thank you son for all the joy you give to my heart.

My Gentle Giant

Love the Lord, all his saints. The Lord preserves the faithful, but the proud he pays back in full. Be strong and take heart, all you who hope in the Lord.

Psalms 31:23-24

When we lost Janet we felt as if our life and our ministry to our children was over. We just couldn't do it anymore. Our hearts hurt. We were physically, mentally and emotionally drained. God had a different plan. Less than one year later Cody Alexander came into our lives. What a sweet salve to the open wounds of our hearts.

Cody came to us on medication for Post Traumatic Stress Disorder. We were told that he may have witnessed acts of violence as an infant. It was believed that he had sensory integration issues. I do not have a lot of information about his birth mom or his father. I just feel saddened by the unstable start he got in life. Cody spent several months in foster care before coming into our home. As we all know that is not always the most pleasant experience either.

Cody has been in our home for two and a half years now. He has been off all medication since six months after his arrival and is doing well. He receives speech and occupational therapy. These seem to have helped a lot with the sensory issues. He also attends play therapy.

My sweet son struggles daily with fear, insecurity and anger. He requires constant reassurance of our love and commitment to him. He is growing and becoming more secure every day.

Daily he brings joy to our lives. He laughs, plays and sings. Cody is learning more every day. I am amazed at the joy he finds in every day life. All of life is a treasure waiting to be discovered. In Cody's world a simple pine cone becomes a pet porcupine, a rock a small turtle named Gus. His laughter fills our home and most of all my heart.

Sometimes it seems that he is growing right before my eyes. He is certainly a very normal little boy. God's healing power in his life is obvious to all who are watching him grow.

What joy fills my heart when he runs to me with his arms stretched wide. Cody is talking up a storm now and loves to tell me everything about his day. It is a miracle we see when we look at him. God has taken so much of the fear from his heart. He has allowed Cody to bond with us. Trust is a gift that has been given to us. Cody thinks mommy can fix anything. He runs to me and tells on everyone.

Every gift that someone gives him is a treasure and he cries if it is lost. He treasures all those people he has learned to trust. When I look into those big brown eyes I see God's goodness and compassion. Cody has been my comfort. God has used him in my life to bring healing and restore my faith. He has taught me to open my heart and love once again.

He has grown and is much larger than typical three year olds. When he runs to me for hugs he often knocks me down. We frequently lie there on the floor and laugh together. I am still getting to know Cody and He is still learning about me, but we are certainly connected at the heart. I look at my Gentle Giant and realize that his size is a mere reflection of the heart he has for others.

His creativity never fails to amaze me. Whether he is going into character as a lion or molding alligators from foil wrappers he always has a captive audience. His love for nature, animals and all of God's creation is a picture into his heart. Every element of life is a treasure to him.

I pray that as we grow together as a family that God will fill any void that Cody might feel from the loss of his biological family. My request is that God will grant Cody the ability to grow in the grace and the knowledge of our Lord and that he will know the love of his heavenly father in such a way that he will want for nothing.

Cody will grow to be a man of God. I already see his love for Jesus. I have dried many tears when he was ill and could not go to church. As I listen to his sweet voice utter his prayers at night I am reminded that there is but one thing that is important. When we go to our father and hold out our arms to Him we will be held and all things put right.

I thank God every day for the honor of being his mommy. When I lay down at night I can trust God to protect my family. I go to sleep with peace in my heart. Once again the light of a joyful morning has been granted after a very long and painful night.

A Love Letter to my Savior

For so long I felt forsaken and alone
like a wander with no home.
Then you came into my heart
and tore it all apart.

You swept away the guilt and shame
And made me pure and whole again.
You chased away the fear
and dried every tear.

You told me of a love so sweet and true
I eagerly found myself running to you.
Now I lay all my burdens at the foot of the cross
Counting all the blessing your love has bought.
Thank you father full of love
Thank you Savior for your grace.
Thank you Holy Spirit for taking fear and
uncertainty and leaving joy in it's place.
Praise you for giving a weary woman rest.
Praise you for leaving me feeling blessed.

The Angels of My Heart

We wait in hope for the Lord; he is our help and our shield. In him our hearts rejoice, for we trust in his holy name. May your unfailing love rest upon us, O Lord, even as we put our hope in you.

Psalms 33:20-22

As we travel down life's road and experience what life offers, we often miss the most important and obvious blessings. This is the story of the road I walked down, the blessings I failed to see, and how I was carried back home on the wings of angels. It is a story of lessons learned and faith strengthened.

I was born in Maryville, Tennessee in 1969. Growing up in the south gave me many beautiful memories to carry into adulthood. My mother worked hard as a nurse to care for me and my two younger brothers. My father was never a part of my life. As a result, I struggled with feelings of inadequacy. If my father couldn't love me who could? Growing up in the Bible Belt church was a huge part of my life. My brothers and I would ride the bus to church every Sunday morning. The highlight of my week was singing songs with all the kids on the bus. I remember listening to my Sunday school teachers and children's church leaders talk about Jesus and how much He loved me, enough to die for me_ I could not understand how my Heavenly Father could love me enough to give His only son for me.

I am not totally sure I comprehend it now. All I knew at that age was awe and wonder over the fact that I was not fatherless, I had a father in Heaven who loved me and cherished me. I accepted Jesus into my heart at the tender age of six. I always hungered to hear His word and to be with people who loved God and would teach me more about Him. As I grew older I became discouraged at the difficulties and disappointments in life.

I left home at eighteen thinking I had all the answers. I didn't. I married a man who was 10 years older than me. It did not take long to realize that he had a serious alcohol problem. When he drank he became abusive in every sense of the word. Two years later I returned to my mother's home. I had a failed marriage behind me and a beautiful daughter by my side. I lived with my mother and brothers for several month. After getting my CNA certification I was able to move out on my own. It was a struggle trying to raise an infant and work, but my family was there for me. Elizabeth and I cherished our time together and began the healing process.

Some time later I was reunited with my high school sweetheart. When we had dated in high school I had been convinced that we would marry someday. But like most high school love affairs it was short lived. When things ended I was extremely disappointed

We were married in September of 1989. The three of us were a ready made family. Greg got accepted to Air Traffic Control School. Although this required him to move to Oklahoma City for three months we felt we were living a fairy tale. We started our family with the highest of hopes and the largest of dreams.

I became pregnant very quickly. Time passed swiftly and our excitement grew right along with my belly. We had no resignations. I walked around for several weeks with my head in the clouds. Little did I know that my dream was soon to be shattered. I awoke one night in a cold sweat and hurting badly. I was sure I was feeling contractions, but I was only five and a half months pregnant.

Alone and afraid, I called a friend to take me to the hospital. I was given medicine through an IV drip in an attempt to stop my labor. After a futile attempt I was told there was nothing else that could be done to stop my labor. At three in the morning I gave birth to a very small lifeless baby boy. Although my husband and I grieved our loss, we never had a funeral, or even a memorial service.

It wasn't until years later that we named our little son. We had failed to see the importance of his little life and his death. No matter how short a child's life, it's very purpose is to add quality and blessing to our own lives. Our son Kenneth Job brought many blessings into our heart that at the time we chose to overlook.

Several years passed and along with it many more failed pregnancies. Soon our hopes began to dwindle. Although we were a family with great faith things seem to look dim.

In September of 1992 we were expecting again. We watched the months pass without much hope in our hearts of this pregnancy becoming a reality. In the beginning of my fifth month we had an ultrasound, and to our surprise we were told that there were two babies. Twins, we were going to have twins. They were both boys.

My husband was in shock. I was excited. We both felt that our hope had returned. This time things were going to be different. We began to look forward to the future.

Later into my fifth month, I began to experience mild cramping and felt uncomfortable. I went to see the doctor, thinking it was probably a mild urinary tract infection.

I was informed that one of my babies was already detached from the uterine wall and the other partially detached. Neither of them had a heartbeat. So in March of 1993 we grieved the death of our two infant sons, Jacob Gregory and Zachary Guy. One month later we lost my grandmother to liver cancer. I cannot begin to tell you how crushed we were. I believe that is when I stepped onto the slippery slope that we all try to avoid.

Once again our future seemed very sad and we were unsure of ourselves. I became severely depressed. Our family began to go through several changes. My husband Greg became withdrawn and we stopped communicating our feelings to one another. When we did talk we only argued. We could not seem to recover our joy. Very regretfully our precious little girl Beth got lost in our misery. She must have felt so confused and alone.

In our misery we could not recognize God at work in our lives. One day a good friend came to us and asked if we had considered adoption. She told us about a little boy with Cerebral Palsy who needed a forever family. Suddenly we found ourselves looking into our hearts. Could we love an adopted child unconditionally? Would this child feel like our own? Could we accept him without fear and judgement? Could God bring healing to us through this child? Most importantly was this how God intended to build our family? After much prayer we decided to apply to adopt that little boy.

We rushed around and did all that was asked of us and settled in for the wait. Boy was it a difficult wait. Every time the phone rang my heart skipped a beat. Every time the mail ran I was the first to the box. The answer seemed to take forever. When it finally came it wasn't exactly what we had prayed for.

We were informed that another family had been chosen for him. Yet another disappointment for our little family, but at the same time we felt amazed at seeing God's hand on this little one's life.

But now I was a woman on a mission. We wanted a big, happy family and God had shown me a way that it could happen. His solutions are always perfect. What I had not counted on was the fact that His timing may not be my timing. We finished our home study and got on a waiting list with a local adoption agency. We rushed around getting forms filled out, and met with a social worker who interviewed us. Then she interviewed our family, our friends, our pastor, and our friend's pastor, etc. Then we played the waiting game.

We waited, and waited, and waited some more. For a total of two and a half years we waited. Thinking that all was lost and that maybe we had misread God's will for our family, we became discouraged. Greg couldn't cope anymore. He asked for a transfer back to our home town.

Once again our disbelief got in the way of our faith. It turns out that God's timing was exactly one month before we were scheduled to leave. Our social worker called to tell us we had a baby girl. Imagine our surprise at having this blessing come to us in a time of tremendous transition for our family. Greg began to doubt if we were doing the right thing at the right time in our life. But God worked in his heart and made His will obvious.

So, on June 14, 1994, Suzanna Elaine came kicking and screaming into our lives. Suzanna had been born thirteen week premature and had various medical needs. Never the less she stole our hearts, and we went forth with blind faith. We moved to Tennessee only to find that it was not where God wanted us to be. We had made a decision on our own without God's approval and we were paying the price for our disobedience. We amassed hundreds of dollars in medical bills, our house was broken into several times and my husband and I were feeling further apart than ever.

We were getting the message loud and clear that we needed to be back in North Carolina where we belonged. So, we went. Immediately we could sense that we were where God wanted us to be.

In February of 1996 God sent us another blessing. He sent us a son, Evan Gregory. Evan was born with a genetic disorder. Once again God seemed to be calling us to higher ground. We began to feel that adoption had been God's will for our family from the beginning.

When we finally submitted to His will for our lives amazing things began to happen. Three years later Katie Ann came into our lives. Katie was also born early. She had fluid built up around her brain and required a shunt. What we learned about Katie was that her family had planned to abort her. But, God had a different plan and after an emergency surgery to deliver her she was placed in our family. What a blessing.

Several years later Janet Marie was grafted into our lives. Little did we know what God had planned for our family_ Our amazing journey with her was short but precious. She was the glue that cemented us together as a family. God used her life to teach me about unconditional love and His amazing grace.

Shortly after Janet went to be with Jesus God dried our tears and quieted our weeping. He brought joy back into our lives in the form of a two year old. What a sweet salve Cody Alexander has been to our aching hearts. His beauty and laughter fill our home with joy.

Beth has grown to be a beautiful, healthy young woman, who is now moving into her own role as a young woman and maybe one day a mom. As I watch her grow and develop into the young woman God wants her to be I utter a prayer of thanksgiving. I thank God for not allowing our pain, depression and lack of faith to destroy her beautiful spirit.

Now, as I look back, I see all that happened in our lives had a purpose and a blessing. We had laughed and cried together. We grieved and celebrated together. But the most important thing is that we did it *together*.

As I look back on the events of our lives together I see that they were the fibers that held us firmly together in the times we felt the furthest apart. I see that although the loss of our babies hurt and changed our lives forever, they also made us *real* and *alive*. They opened us up to God's will.

It was the worst thing to happen to us, and yet it was the best. Although it was hard to say good-bye when most parents are saying hello it awakened in us a truer love, a meaningful, unconditional love.

Someone once told me that the heart doesn't break all at once, it breaks slowly, piece by piece. Our hearts had to be broken in order to open us up to accept God's leadership in our lives. We now have six beautiful children who have filled us with joy. We know that each one was God sent and a blessed gift to us.

All of them were the angels that carried me home. They brought me home to the true meaning of love and family. God took my life, as broken and empty as it was and used it to his glory. Every day, as I watch my family grow and develop, I am awed at the grace of my Lord and Savior. God replaced that emptiness with a house and a heart full of joy.

It is difficult to watch the people that I love go through trials. At times the illnesses, surgeries and procedures overwhelm me. At times I am terrified that God chose the wrong person to do this. Just when I get to the end of that proverbial rope I can feel God's protective hand reach down and pull me back up. The strength returns and He carries me through whatever is happening at the time. People ask me all the time how we do all there is to do. We take one step at a time and pray without ceasing.

I no longer feel the loss of my earthly father as deeply as I did as a child. The everlasting, unconditional love of my heavenly father fills that void. When I am afraid I cry out to Him and he wraps me in His love. Our trials and our hardships are not to punish us. They are allowed in our life to help us grow. They strengthen us and equip us to do what God has planned.

Daily I find myself seeking opportunities to get alone with God. I will not tell you that life is ordinary or simple, it is actually far from it. I also will not lead you to believe that I do not question God. At times I still struggle with depression, feelings of inadequacy, and I will probably always feel the deep sadness of our losses. But I know that my God is in control. He is teaching me to let go and allow Him to work. There is such freedom in knowing that I don't have to do it alone. As a mother my experiences vary from day to day. I have learned that my happiness cannot be based on my circumstances. My happiness is founded in my Lord and Savior.

He loved me so much that He shed His blood for me_ How can you feel alone and inadequate with that knowledge? Faith is more than saying you believe in something. Hebrews 11:1 tells us that Faith means being sure of the things we hope for and knowing that something is real even if we do not see it. God has used my family to teach me Faith, unconditional love and forgiveness.

In my darkest moments He has given light. He allowed me my night of weeping but faithfully brought a joyful morning.

Reflections of
the Heart

10/18/03

Janet,

As we begin our journey I want you to know how much you have enriched my life. I know I cannot take away the hurts of a time past. All I can do is hope to fill all your to morrows with love and fun. I love you so much it fills my heart to overflowing.

I hang on every sound you make and treasure every sweet smile. I long for it when it is not there. When you awake at three or four in the morning crying and saying "ooom" it makes me leap from my bed and run to you. I love you now and forever.

Love,
Mommy

11/20/03

Janet,

Each day you are growing and learning. Something they said you were incapable of. It is amazing to me that you look for each of us as you hear our name called. It is more amazing when you smile at something funny or respond to a toy or a song. We knew when we saw you for the very first time on the internet site for children waiting to be adopted that you were a miracle. We never expected that God would bless us so richly and make you OUR miracle.

I am so sorry that I have no ability to change the past. I am equally sorry for every bad thing and every rejection you have suffered at the hands of people who should have protected you. I can only make every day from here on a blessing. I will not reject you. You are my daughter and I love you. Through the good, the bad and unbelievable we will stay together until the end. That is my promise to you darling.

Love,
Mommy

12/6/03

Dear Janet,

Today is your birthday. We had a party for you. You slept through every thing but the cake and ice cream. It is so amazing that you are eating when three months ago you were totally tube fed. You didn't know what to do with a spoon.

I am so proud of you honey. You work so hard at every challenge. I am so blessed to share this day with you.

Love,
Mommy

12/25/03

Dear Janet,

This was your first Christmas with us and the excitement danced in your eyes. You were so alert today and aware that today was different from any other day.

Joy shone on you little face. It radiated out to us all. It was the most blessed Christmas we have ever had. You lay beneath the tree smiling and sharing secrets with the lights on the tree. You have shown us joy in the simple things. Thank you my darling for such a wonderful and loving gift. Probably the best Christmas present I have ever received. I love you.

Love,
Mommy

Dear Janet,

You are not feeling very well these past few days. You are sleeping more and more. I took you to your pulmonologist today. He ordered some tests as well as your pediatrician. Your temperatures are running low. (94 and lower) They need to find out why. Don't worry honey it is going to be okay. Jesus loves you and I know He is working in your life. He will help the doctors find out what is going on. I love you and pray daily for your health and happiness.

Love,
Mommy

Dear Janet,

Today Ms. Kim came to draw blood for the doctors. She could not get the blood. We could not even find a vein. She will come back in two days and try again. She has asked that we increase your fluid intake in hopes of hydrating you more. Perhaps that will allow us to get what is needed. I am trying to be brave but it is so hard when you have been sleeping most of the time for the past two days and we cannot keep your temp up. No one can tell us why yet.

I bought you an electric blanket for when you are up and in your chair during the day. I hope it will help. Honey, this is a hard time but we are going to get through it together. I made you a promise and no matter how hard things get we are a family and families stay together.

God is so evident in your little life. He is watching over you always. You are such a miracle and never doubt that you are a blessing.

Love,
Mommy

1/14/04

Dear Janet,

Today we had a CAT scan. I am fearful of what it may find. One thing I know is that we need answers. I want you to be well cared for and to do those things you need. I love you and no matter what this shows, we will face it together. My only prayer is that you wont be afraid. I know that so much has happened in your life that has been scary. Especially because most of the time you were going through it alone. I promise that will never happen again. I promise we will be there for you always. I am blessed that you are my daughter.

Love,
Mommy

1/15/04

Dear Janet,

Today we traveled to Greenville, SC to see a Neurology specialist. He told us that calcium deposits were building in your brain. Over one half of your hypothalamus is calcified. That is why your temperature has been out of control. It is a relief to know this, but I am so sad that there is nothing we can do. We will keep praying for a miracle. Don't give up Janey, God is in control. I love you.

Love,
Mommy

1/16/04

Dear Janet,

Where do I begin? My heart is so heavy. Your doctor called today and discussed the CT scan. Oh, Honey, all I want to do is cry.

The scan showed that all of your brain tissue has died. Your brainstem function is all that is keeping you alive.

He told us that any day you may stop breathing_ There is nothing we can do. He says you are terminally ill. Janet, I want you to know that even if we only have a short time together you have filled me with a lifetime of joy. Don't feel for a minute that you have been a burden on us. You are certainly not.

I love you so much and whether we have a day, a week, or years left may be undetermined but we have already bonded together as mother and daughter. You have made my life rich. You have taught me so much about God's love and faithfulness. You will never know how grateful I am for the wonderful life lessons you have taught me.

I love you my sweet angel daughter. You are my hero, beautiful child of my heart.

Love,
Mommy

1/17/04

Dear Janet,

Janey, today has been a hard day. You had two really bad seizures and one small one. I feel so helpless and you look so scared. Honey I hate knowing you are scared and in pain. I pray God's mercy and healing for you. I pray for strength and courage to face each day. I also pray He will show me what to do and how to love you completely every day. Baby, please don't be scared. Mommy and Daddy love you and so does God.

Love,
Mommy

Dear Janet,

Today has been a good day. You ate for me today. You had a seizure free day and were happy all day. Every time I looked at you I saw a huge smile on your face. You cooed and babbled.

It was like music to my ears. The song "I Can Only Imagine" by Mercy Me came on and you were singing it with your heart. Thank you for blessing me with your sweet spirit and beautiful smile.

Love,
Mommy

PS. Today it rained, but after there was a rainbow in the sky. God's promise... Don't forget.

2/4/04

My Dear sweet girl,

What joy you bring to my heart. The smile on your face
and in your eyes says all that is hidden in your heart.

I love you so much_ I can see in your eyes you are
beginning to trust us. What joy fills my heart when I
realize the healing that God is putting there.

Love,
Mommy

3/5/04

Dear Janet,

I feel so blessed today. For you see, today is my birthday.
I chose to write to you on my birthday so that you could
know what a wonderful gift from God you are. Today you
tried to laugh out loud. What a beautiful sound. Thank
you for such a wonderful gift.

Love,
Mommy

4/6/04

Sweetheart,

You have not been feeling well and blood work has shown us that your sodium levels are low. We will be adjusting your salt intake to help you feel better.

I am praying for you every second of the way.

Be strong and know that Jesus loves you and will never leave you alone.

I love you

Love,
Mommy

5/3/04

Dear Janet,

Things are so hard lately. You seem to struggle so hard every day. We are doing cough assist twice a day to keep your lungs clear and you are now on a Bi-Pap ventilator at night. There are so many medications and you are on oxygen about eight hours a day every day now. You have good and bad days.

You also have a lot of bad nights. It hurts me to see you this way. I pray every day for a miracle. I love you and wish I could take it all away.

Love,
Mommy

6/11/04

Honey,

Today was a rough day. I have tried to get your oxygen
level up but you are struggling so hard_ Sometimes I
feel as if God isn't hearing my prayers_ I pray anyway. I
don't know what else to do. I am trying so hard to keep it
together here. I know you are too. I love you.

Love,
Mommy

6/12/04

Dear Janet,

I am so scared. You are looking so pale and having such a hard time. The doctor is advising us and everyone is doing what we can for you. I hear all the junk in your lungs and I am terrified. I don't know what else to do. I love you and will stay close to you at all times.

Love,
Mommy

6/13/04

Honey,

Today has been horrible. You are struggling to breath and your oxygen levels are 60-70 percent. The doctor had a second oxygen compressor brought out. It is not helping. Baby, I don't know what to say. I love you and it is killing me to see you struggle this hard. We are all praying for you.

Love,
Mommy

6/14/04

My Sweet Baby,

You are gone now and I have a hole in my heart. I ache so badly and miss you terribly. I heard you at four thirty this morning and came to you. Your oxygen level was 47 percent. I felt my heart breaking. I knew then it was time to say good-bye. Daddy and I woke the other kids, Nanna, Beth, Tammy, and Teresa. We all talked to you and I was able to hold you and be with you til the end.

But I am not ready to say good-bye. I hurt so bad. I will miss you so much. I know you are with Jesus and this gives me peace, but oh, how I will miss you. My day has been filled with things I did not want to do. Making arrangements. As I sat on your bed and dressed you for the final time my mind flashed back to the many times I have bathed and dressed you, although your expression did not change, in my heart I could see your smile.

It has been such an honor to be your mommy, even if it was for such a short time. I love you my darling. I will never forget the way it felt to cradle you close to me, or the sound of your sweet coo when you were singing. Your smile will be forever imprinted on my heart. You have taught me so much. You have made me a stronger person by making me more dependent on God.

You have taught me to slow down and just enjoy being with you. You taught us all to love in a deeper way than I ever imagined was possible. Thank you for sharing your beauty with us, if only for a short while. I love you my darling. I know you know that but I want to say it again and again. We have lived and loved a lifetime in nine short months. Our time together was precious and will be treasured in my heart forever. Good-bye, my little angel, for now. But yet a while and we will be reunited in Heaven with our lord and savior. Now as always I am entrusting you to Him.

All my love.
Forever your Mommy

www.ingramcontent.com/pod-product-compliance
Lightning Source LLC
Chambersburg PA
CBHW051642120626
46551CB00015B/2187